Stop Procrastinating Now!

How to end procrastination once and for all

Steven T. Walker

Galatea Editions

Stop Procrastinating Now! How to end procrastination once and for all, by Steven T. Walker.

© Steven T. Walker 2021
© Galatea Editions 2021
© All rights reserved

Thank you for buying this book. The copyright is exclusive property of the author, therefore, the reproduction, copying and distribution of this book are not allowed, whether it's for commercial or non-profit purposes.

If this manual was useful to you, I'd really appreciate it if you could rate it on Amazon. Your support helps me continue writing.

Index

PROLOGUE 7
INTRODUCTION 16
TYPES OF PROCRASTINATION 18
   MONETARY PROCRASTINATION 18
   MEDICAL PROCRASTINATION 20
   OTHER TYPES OF PROCRASTINATION: 22
PROCRASTINATION, A MONSTER WITH MANY FACES. 24
   PERFECTIONISM 24
   FEAR OF DISAPPOINTING 25
   REJECTION TOWARDS AUTHORITY 26
STRATEGIES TO FIGHT PROCRASTINATION 29
   MAKE LISTS: 31
   WHAT IS A SPIRAL OF SUCCESS? 33
   ESTABLISHING A FRAME FOR WORK 35
   RESIST TEMPTATIONS 36
   POMODORO TECHNIQUE 38
   ADMINISTER YOUR ENERGIES 40
   GET INSPIRED BY TRIUMPHANT PEOPLE AND FOLLOW IN THE FOOTSTEPS 42
   FIND GROUPS THAT POWER YOUR SKILLS 43
   WHAT IS AN *ACCOUNTABILITY BUDDY*? 45
      Advice: 46
   REWARD YOURSELF FOR YOUR TRIUMPHS 47
   RETHINK WHAT WE DO 50
   CREATE NEW HABITS 53
   USE PROCRASTINATION TO YOUR ADVANTAGE 57
   SMALL OBSTACLES 59
CONCLUSION 61

Prologue

Before we talk about procrastinating, and delving deep into a subject that is having so much relevance nowadays, I'd like to start off with a short story that will accompany us throughout the whole book.

Two journalist writers, who used to work four hours a day at a comfortable office downtown, were forced into taking one hour daily so they could get to work in time, where they worked making phone calls and writing news for as long as their shifts lasted, and another extra hour to take the public transportation so they could get back home.

With that workflow, they both managed to write an average of three weekly news stories, which were published in a *newsletter* format each Saturday; until, suddenly, a pandemic completely modified their daily routine.

To prevent their employees from taking the risk of catching the virus, they were given the opportunity to work from home, thus preventing the exposure to public transportation and spending around four hours a day sharing the space of a tight office.

The only thing they were asked, was that every Friday, they submitted the three articles that corresponded to a week's amount of work. A similar pace to the one they were already used to. At the beginning, all of the workers felt comfortable and grateful, since this meant they could manage their time better, work more efficiently and even have more free time.

One of our lead characters, let's call him "Prometheus", started to get amazing results from week one. Faithful to his habits, he continued to wake up at 6 in the morning and after having breakfast and taking care of his personal hygiene, instead of taking the public transportation, he started the work for his weekly articles.

In this way, his work shift started an hour earlier, and it elongated an hour further than what he was used to, since he didn't have to take the bus back home either.

And just like that, the week's work started to be ready on Wednesdays or Thursdays, making Prometheus enjoy new liberties to carry on his university education, do sports at home, reading novels, and many other activities he could not perform with his previous work schedule. Without a doubt, the change in his schedule and the new work flexibilization modality made his life substantially change for the better.

In time, he even started working on writing a book, an activity he knew he had the potential and the skill to perform, thanks to so many years of experience writing all kinds of texts.

This is how he decided to take advantage of all that extra time to carry out his first publications in an efficient way, which will allow him to enjoy a better economic stability.

Prometheus was the worker that I thought I would become. Sadly, Prometheus didn't exist until many months had passed and many failures had been accumulated.

The truth is things didn't turn out to be so easy after I started with the *home office*. I still remember that first Monday when the alarm went off. Logic indicated that, if I had been able to get up at 6 in the morning for so many years to get to the office on time, I could do the same thing when it came to working from home.

Instead, the first thing I thought was, since I didn't have the obligation to make it on time at 8 in the morning, I could sleep for an extra hour; so the choice I made was sleeping till 7.

When I woke up again at 7, it was time to get going. But instead of starting quickly with my activities, I stayed in bed for a couple more minutes. I took my time checking my emails, and my social media, but after a while a brilliant idea came to mind.

By working from home, not only was I saving an hour of transport to go to the office, but I was also gaining an extra hour, the one from the trip back. This is how I decided to sleep again, a second extra hour.

When I finally got up, and after taking a shower and having breakfast, I realized that even if I was already late on my shift, there was no one to control me. Even if I had always been able to make it on time before my weekly submission deadline, I didn't have any reason to feel pressured. After all, this was the first day of the rest of my life, a window that was going to allow me to transition into success and a better lifestyle. I thought I deserved to finish my breakfast in peace, watch the news, and after that start working.

After catching up with everything that was going on in the country and the world, I was ready to sit before the computer and start writing. But, instead of opening Drive and creating a new text document, I started by opening Facebook, Instagram, and then I moved on to YouTube to listen to some music.

Just like that, I worked more unfocused than ever, time seemed infinite, so I made sure I checked the results of the Football League and also the Formula 1.

After long hours of doing nothing, came the moment of tending to my following obligations, which is why I closed the blank document and logged on to my virtual classes. Then I dedicated the rest of the afternoon to my university studies. That was my first day working from home, it was completely sterile but I didn't feel the slightest bit of guilt; my work wasn't all that difficult and I could fulfill my weekly quota on the following days.

The second day was not much different from the first. Only that, on this occasion, I had already set up the alarm so I could sleep without interruptions until 9 in the morning.

Once I was up, I took a shower, I had some breakfast and once again, I invested almost an extra hour reading the news before I started my work shift.

But it was Tuesday, and once again, excuses were stronger than obligations. It had been a long time since I last cleaned my home, and now that I had to work in it, it was just necessary that I kept it in optimal conditions. Which is why I carefully tidied up each corner, even if I decided to throw away all the stuff I didn't use anymore afterwards. I checked the woodshed, and my closet, I threw away my old clothes and, when everything was squeaky clean, I sat down so I could get going with my work. However, since the light was coming in through a hole in my old curtains, I decided to use the last hour before my online classes to go get some new curtains. For the second day in a row, I postponed my daily work.

That same night, I organized a poker game with some friends I hadn't seen in a while. I had reached them all during work hours on different social media. The game extended longer than anticipated, and I stayed there until the chips and the beers ran out anyways.

After all, I just had to write three articles that generally took me about 6.3 hours each on average. If during the mornings of Wednesday, Thursday and Friday I started waking up at 6 in the morning again, and I managed to dedicate the six hours of work that I had to invest on writing the articles, everything should have been done by Friday.

But I slept past the alarm on Wednesday. I went to bed at 5:15 a.m. and I didn't notice the alarm clock went off and rang tirelessly at 6:00, 6:05, 6:10 and 6:15.

When I finally woke up to the sunlight at noon, everything started turning uphill. The morning shower was suspended, breakfast I had over the computer so I couldn't really enjoy it. The ideas didn't seem to come to my head, which was clouded, terrorized by the passing of time, and it started to drive me crazy.

My phone kept ringing and all I could think about was that it was my bosses, asking for updates of my work. The computer seemed to go slower than usual, and the interviews I had to do weren't available, something that, though it was quite common, required me to re-schedule them, which I didn't have the time to do.

There was no margin to maneuver, I had to do everything quickly and I had to get back the missing time, but everything was turning difficult.

By the end of the day, in which the hours didn't suffice like I wanted them to, all the activities had a bitter taste. I took my virtual classes with guilt, thinking that I could have been making up for the lost time. I even modified my night routine, since I was used to running, reading a book, or watching a movie before going to sleep.

But since I felt like I was running out of time, that I was in a rush and that I didn't deserve it, I put aside these activities, with the excuse that, if I went to bed early, I could recover the lost time the next morning.

But I couldn't sleep. Every 15 minutes I checked the same things on my cell phone: Instagram, Facebook, YouTube, News, nothing had changed, and the minutes kept moving forward.

I moved around on the bed, I tried to sleep again, but the cycle repeated every 15 minutes: Instagram, Facebook, YouTube, News. Everything was the same, but I was already running late again, I had to sleep. Finally, after checking my cell phone three more times, I got to sleep for a couple of hours.

On the next day, I tried to work at a pace that allowed me to recover the missing time, but once more, I didn't have breakfast properly and coordinating the interviews was not an easy task.

I managed to finish the first article, but I didn't even bother to proofread it, since I quickly started the next one. I was writing fast, I looked for whoever was available, I moved forward with new interviews and I did what was possible to recover the missing time.

I didn't have time to finish the second article before I started my online classes, which is why I minimized Zoom and I just listened to what was being said in the background while I finished my work. Of course, it was little help. Not only was I not writing at 100% of my ability, but I didn't listen to a single word of the class. "I'll listen to it on the weekend", I said to myself as I wrote to my supervisor letting him know that I was posting my first two articles.

On Friday, when I was about to start writing my third and last article, I read a message that my supervisor had sent me. It was quite lengthy, but long story short, he told me not to bother writing the third article, and that I should use my time on Friday to correct and work harder on my first two ones, which were very low quality. Finally, he told me to make up for the undelivered work from this week, on the following week.

It wasn't easy to start the day off with such a call to attention, or knowing that I was still behind on my articles and classes, and that next week, I'd have even more work.

After investing long hours, with a much lower performance than I was used to, I managed to deliver the first two articles, but to do this I had to skip class again. This time, I didn't even bother to open Zoom.

I was feeling so much guilt that I chose to not watch any movies once more, nor to go out running, thinking about the classes I had to make up for. But, since the weekend was long, I didn't set myself up to get going.

The following week, I repeated my new vices, I was sleeping in till late, living with guilt, I didn't go out running because I couldn't afford spending time doing so, but my time in front of the screen was becoming less and less productive.

I was writing during my virtual classes, I thought about my career as I worked. On the other hand, I got distracted with social media and banal, repetitive games, since I thought they would take less time from me than working out, reading or watching a movie.

At university they started programming the dates of the exams, and obviously, along with them came the bad grades, since I lived postponing my studies. At work, they kept calling out my mediocre performance, I couldn't sleep at night and I set up the alarm earlier and earlier, though this didn't translate into more work hours.

That was how I failed that semester, I didn't manage to invest a single moment on the book I always wanted to write and I was forced to come into the office again and fulfill my work schedule there, this as retaliation for my latest, and poorest articles.

I realized that I had lost a golden opportunity. The opportunity to be Prometheus, to move forward with my objectives with strength and to improve the quality of my life.

It took a couple of months for me to recover the life that I used to have. The company's psychologist helped me a lot and recommended that I go back to my reading, working out, and to set a schedule for my social media.

After a lot of work, I managed to build new habits that allowed me to improve my working and study time, and the hours of the day.

On a personal level, I was lucky that my supervisor's patience wasn't infinite and that he forced me to gain control of my steady work. But when we speak of those activities that nobody forces you to do, the situation can get to be a lot more serious.

When what you really want to do is something that depends only on you, and there's nobody to motivate you to move forward, whether it is writing a book, starting your own business, or simply asking that girl you like out, that's when procrastinating becomes really dangerous.

There are those who spend their entire life postponing their dreams, and when they realize that the deadline is close, it's far too late. They realize that little by little, their youth, years, and life passed by, just because they couldn't decide to get going.

Introduction

The first thing we must do before talking about how to avoid procrastination, or to learn some strategies that we could apply to get free of its claws, is to know in detail what is known as procrastinating.

Even if the word comes from the Latin "pro", which means "ahead of" and "crastinos", which means "tomorrow", that literal definition from centuries ago was becoming more and more complex and encompassing.

Many times, life itself demands from us a little bit of patience, self-control and to postpone activities under a priority list. Which in a literal sense, means that we procrastinate.

But in the last few centuries, the word started to gain new circulation and importance and it was because of a small adjustment that was made to its definition, which transformed a word comparable to "waiting" into a much more negative concept, which would be "postponing tasks in a voluntary way, despite being conscious that said postponing will be prejudicial in the future".

Which means, it's not just about simply waiting, like those who move their morning workout to the evening, so they don't suffer from the excessive heat. But, to be considered procrastinating, we must be acting against that which we know is convenient for us.

For instance, knowing that studying ahead of time for an exam will allow us to be more prepared and have more spare time later in the future, and still not doing it, damaging ourselves.

Even if we're capable of making it on time everywhere, in part, it could be considered as procrastination. Many times, just so that we don't start doing those tasks that are boring, or stressful to us, like sweeping the house, watering the plants, or running some errands, we excuse ourselves saying that we're too busy to do them, so we leave early for work or any other commitments.

In this way, we can grab a coffee, talk to colleagues, check our social media and dilate the times a little bit without feeling guilty over the tasks that we're not fulfilling.

In this situation, we're also procrastinating. Because even if we did those things that are priorities, before the deadline, we're still putting off tasks and responsibilities that may not be as important, but that sooner or later we'll have to do.

This is how procrastination is not only about postponing our tasks and responsibilities, but about an attitude that doesn't allow us to be as productive as we could be. When we are capable of excusing ourselves to avoid moving forward with tasks that we consider necessary and that, in the long run, they'll start weighing in on us.

Types of procrastination

Even if the idea of procrastination is one, there are different ways in which it can affect our lives, each and every one of them are consequences that can be more or less corrosive depending on multiple factors.

Meaning, if you're a millionaire, having a delay on your taxes and paying overcharges in some receipts may not be as damaging to your lifestyle as dilating the time that you should dedicate to your family or health. But this will depend on each person, which means that, without saying which kind of procrastination weighs more than the other, I will simply mention some of the most common types.

Monetary procrastination

The monetary procrastination happens when our procrastinating vice starts causing economic problems that affect our financial stability, or that simply doesn't allow us to make as much money as we could.

A very common case, that repeats itself on those graduated from the different colleges is that they never take the time to make their thesis, hence, even if they invested 5 or 6 years of their lives studying in the university, they dilate their time for presenting their final work so much, that in many cases, some miss out on getting paid the additional money that comes with the title.

After all, they already have a job that relates to their profession and the thesis can be presented at any moment. Unfortunately, that moment which could very well be this semester, is usually programmed for next year, and then the next one, and then the next one.

The same thing usually happens with the people who wish to start their own businesses or work in an independent way. Since we're dealing with tasks that we can start at any moment, a lot of people feel the tranquility of knowing they don't have an obligation to get it done quickly, which means they can always wait a little bit longer to be sufficiently prepared.

Let's imagine for a second that we want to open our own bicycle shop. We think of the basic needs we must be able to solve and we buy all that's needed to do so, maybe some patches, replacement chambers, tools, a pump, amongst other elements.

When we think we're all set, maybe we start questioning whether we're sufficiently prepared or not, then we dedicate an additional month to take YouTube classes and learn new techniques that may come in handy.

Once we end our period of preparation, we find out we don't have any items to sell, in case you want to equip your bike. For the customer to leave the store completely pleased, we may need to offer them some stickers, seat covers, horns and accessories.

So, there are those who dilate their time so much that when the moment comes, they manage to equip themselves with all that's necessary, but they're still unable to open their garage's door and pull out a sign to the street offering their bicycle services.

And following this same logic, there are those who postpone their retirement contributions, the payment of their taxes, the beginning of their savings, and many other activities that, if we don't manage to regulate in time, can become highly corrosive to our future.

Medical procrastination

Even if, in the case of the economy, most of its consequences take place in the short or medium-term, we still choose to procrastinate. Let's imagine now the subjects regarding health, where we find a great number of cares and activities that we must perform, and which consequences could take decades to arrive.

It's not that difficult to understand why someone would choose to postpone their medical tests. After all, the situation starts to get stressful when we start thinking of all the previous procedures we have to complete before the end of our routine checks.

Amongst other things, we'd have to call up and make an appointment, this can take over an hour of our time, and the appointment would be set up for, if we're lucky, a month from that moment.

But we would be lucky if it all ended there, since surely, we would need to have more tests done, which means new appointments, procedures, and dates to schedule. And we mustn't forget the most important thing, we'd have to wait a long time for our test results to be ready.

Finally, going back to the doctor so that they can confirm that everything's alright. After all, why wouldn't it be? If we feel completely healthy.

If I probably don't have any diseases, isn't it more convenient to stay at home tending to more important business?

I'll tell you in advance, the answer is no. There are some medical studies and exams we are obliged to get done frequently, at least once a year, which doesn't seem like a long time at all.

Even if it were to take the whole day, during a couple of days, it will still only be two days from an entire year. It's not like you're going to change your life and become a more focused or smarter person just because you dedicate that time that you should use to get checked by the doctor doing other banal activities that come up in your mind as an excuse.

To make matters worse, a procrastinator drags this terrible vice into every single responsibility of their lives, which in many occasions can be an explanation to many pathologies that could've been completely avoided.

For instance, subtleties like making healthy food, going out to run, or even brushing your teeth three times a day. When a person procrastinates, they tend to put other activities first to stop even the most minimal actions that can cause important repercussions on their lives in the future, just for the pleasure of saving up some minutes from activities that seem like a burden to them.

Let's face it, brushing our teeth and flossing, isn't something that demands more than 5 minutes a day. Regardless, these people are a sanitary hazard, and they tend to put short-term pleasure as a priority, instead of looking at the bigger picture that would allow them to analyze how these decisions will affect their lives in the long term. It's not surprising that most people would rather sleep an extra minute than to brush their teeth before going to bed.

But, skipping dental floss is that bad?

To know more about how this can affect our health, I asked my dentist for the worst case he had encountered. He remembered a patient whose teeth were completely covered with a thick layer of tartar. It was so thick that it formed a hard wall. He showed me a photograph and I still think to this day that having agreed to see it wasn't the best idea.

Other types of procrastination:

Despite the fact that I won't delve deep into other types of procrastination -since there are all kinds of it- it's important to mention that every single one of them is a potential risk that threatens our quality of life, at a minimum.

There are lesser aspects where procrastinating can affect our surroundings, despite not even trying to dilate the minutes of our day.

I once met a particular case, a friend who is a procrastinator that, when he needs to use the dishes, he must wash them before, since he has all of his repertoire waiting in the sink. For a moment I thought it was just an isolated case, something that casually happened that time I went visiting him, but no; every time I went over to his place the dishes were bursting out from the sink.

If we look closer into this case, we'll realize that washing a dish, a pot or two, and two forks, demand the same amount of time if we do it before using them than if we do it after we use them. Which means, you're not even saving any time, you're just being forced to live among the dirty dishes just because you're putting off an activity that you're going to have to do anyways.

In the case that you have children or mascots, it's very important that we make an extra effort since our vices are likely to harm other living creatures that, for some reason, trust in us.

If you have a dog, a cat, or a fish, it's very important you remember that their metabolisms work best if they're being fed with a regulated frequency every time, the same amount at the same hour. Also, it's important to remember that among our responsibilities there's the obligation to keep them hygienic, no excuses.

While a pet is usually adorable, in the hands of a procrastinator they can turn into a home's worst enemy, product of their smells, furs, even though there's also the case of those who procrastinate their pet's care, but since they lock them out, they end up being animals with a very pitiful life condition.

If you have a child, the situation becomes even more delicate. In this case, it's not just about feeding, bathing, and caring for them, it's also necessary to play with them, to help them with their homework, to invest a whole lot of time in them. The long-term effects if we procrastinate our responsibilities with a child can be truly sad.

Procrastination, a monster with many faces.

Many times, people who experience procrastination are actually suffering all kinds of fears, and it's these insecurities that lead them to postpone their most important activities.

However, the longer they postpone their activities and obligations, the harder they start to seem, and they often weave an imaginary tangle which makes their fears grow more and more.

Like fear itself was a well in which they had fallen in, and every minute they spent in there, their mind made sure to turn that well into a deeper sediment.

Below, we will go through the profiles of the most common procrastinators, so you can identify if your pathology is the result of one of the following cases; this way, you'll have a greater number of tools that can be useful for reversing this problem. Even if deep within you find peace knowing that there are people out there who struggle with the same worries, this can be useful too.

Perfectionism

One of the most common profiles is the perfectionist, who, as a rule, can't take the idea that a task is being wrongly executed.

These kinds of people, as long as they have the ability to do a perfect job, they'll probably have no problems doing them. Now, when they're faced with a challenge that they know they can't handle with the level of excellence they'd like to, they start making excuses and postponing it.

This is how, postponing these tasks, the perfectionist will continue to remain focused on those activities in which they stand out, collecting perfect results and feeling pleased with themselves. Sadly, we can't put off our last efficient tasks forever, at least not all of them.

Fear of disappointing

Another one of the common causes that hide behind procrastination is the fear of disappointing our bosses, our family and basically all the people who are close to us.

Many times, this fear of not meeting expectations that we believe have been set for us lead us into not doing anything, since we run the risk of disappointing those who believed in us.

At this point, our brain plays against us again, since by putting off our activities the most likely thing to happen is that our fears will slowly start to become a reality, but it won't be due to our lack of ability or talent, but due to the pressure that we often put on ourselves.

There's even a psychological disorder that many times explains this kind of behavior. It's called the "Imposter Syndrome" and it usually happens to those people who tend to minimize and not be fully aware of their full potential, talents and abilities.

That's why when delegating an activity, job position, or very important project to them, they feel like imposters and think that if they continue down that road, they'll be found out and they'll realize that they weren't fit for the job.

Most times, those who suffer from this syndrome are very capable, but insecure people, and since they fear losing what they've achieved, they don't dare keep climbing.

Let's imagine the lifestyle of a university student who passed all their classes and now they just need to present their thesis. If they pass all their classes, it is understood that they're more than capable of doing a presentation with the demanded characteristics. But instead of doing so, they minimize their merits for passing all their classes, they start thinking that passing a class means nothing, and that their entire academic record is not enough to be considered a professional.

Then, they start building a wrong perception that suggests to them that when they present their thesis to the judges, they'll be very disappointed with their performance and automatically retaliate so they don't graduate.

It's obvious that these things don't happen, and the thesis is just another step that any student is capable of performing. But anyway, fear paralyzes them and they start making up new excuses, that's why there's a high percentage of students that never present their thesis.

Rejection towards authority

From all the types of procrastination that exist, rejection towards authority is the most self-destructive one.

It's considered this way, because far from looking for gratification or relieving your stress by postponing activities, when you struggle with rejection towards authority, we do it on purpose, for the plain necessity of contradicting those who are soliciting a work.

In this sense, we can be late to the office, our meetings, deliver our projects with a graceful delay, just so we feel that we're above authority.

Sadly, these small actions that we know can be more destructive for us than for our superiors, and that as much as we rebel, accepting their authority (as long as it's appropriate) is a part of our job, and we'll probably need their approval if we want to keep climbing and conquering better work opportunities.

After all, generally they have a wider view about what it's necessary to do when it comes to work. Surely, we will have a different perception, we'll see priorities in a different way and we'll propose other work alternatives.

But if they're not accepted, we must remember that the final word is theirs, and that throwing tantrums and delivering past the deadlines will do no good. This will only create less trust in you and it will probably make your proposals to be taken less seriously.

Overconfidence in your abilities

If there was one of the many causes that I felt the most related to, is that I had overconfidence in my abilities.

This happened so many times to me that I find it unbelievable that I still fall into the same traps, which consist of thinking that just because your whole life you've been doing certain activities, there is no way you can fail when you face them again.

Since the person has an excessive amount of confidence in their abilities, they can wrongly judge the reach of a certain task, its difficulty level, and the time it would take to do it. Similar to what happened in the experience with which I started this book.

When the moment comes that there aren't any more margins for the slightest mistakes, you'll probably make some and you won't have the chance to fix them on time. If this happens, the level of tension that you'll put yourself through will start rising exponentially, until everything turns into a real mess.

Strategies to fight procrastination

We've reached the most important part. Until now, we've probably talked about things that you already knew and are the reason you started reading this book. This part consists of the different strategies and tricks you can use to make a 360° spin on our lifestyle, and start fighting in an effective way those bad habits that are responsible for the different irregularities in our lives.

For this, the first thing we must do is trust in something bigger than ourselves. It's not a coincidence that all the craziest actions when it comes to strength of will, sacrifice and action were deeds that were made for the name of a larger entity than a simple desire.

For many, it can be a religious belief, a patriotic duty, a nationalist duty, a firm, the wellbeing of a family or simply a personal dream. Every one of these, acts as a north star which we feel the compromise and duty to move towards.

In this sense, we'll have something of bigger importance to put a scale on when we choose between working or taking a rest.

An example of this is when the Greek God Ulysses went through his well-known Odyssey and fought with bravery on the battle of Troy not for him, nor for his self-satisfaction, but he did it to elevate to the highest the name of Ithaca and Greece.

After the war, when thanks to his cleverness they managed to mock the Trojans and claim the victory, and despite of the fact that Poseidon didn't let him return to his land, once again, Ulysses for the name of Ithaca, his kingdom, Penelope, his wife and Telemachus, his son, he takes off on a journey again that took him ten years, where he had to face hundreds of threats. But no matter how difficult the path was, he knew very clearly why he was making his journey and investing so much effort.

This is just one of many examples found in Greek Mythology, like there can be found many others behind every truly worthwhile action. Amongst most of the Olympic athletes, the idea of taking a gold medal home to their countries is often a more worthy idea, which allows them to wake up every morning and continue to train despite the obstacles or not feeling motivated.

This is how in the military doctrines it's often asked that they act on behalf of their flag, the different legal organizations act in the name of the constitution and justice, the workers wake up day after day chasing their salary, thinking of their children's education and their family's happiness.

On the contrary, amongst those who enjoy procrastinating the most, it's often people who still don't have a clear reason as to why they're living, not having found a purpose for their lives still.

This is why, if we want to start activating and channeling all of our energies to fulfill our goals, the first thing we must do is raise our awareness about what will really be our motivation?

It can be something small like a university degree or a job position, or a huge thing like reaching nirvana or founding a hospital. It doesn't matter, but it's necessary that we set a direction which indicates where to walk to, otherwise, we'll be going nowhere, then it's logical that we don't feel like moving.

Like the Uruguayan writer Eduardo Galeano once explained, when he asked himself what the purpose of the utopia was.

"Utopia is on the horizon. I take two steps; she walks away two steps and the horizon moves away ten more steps. Then what's the purpose of utopia? It's that, to walk".

Make lists:

Now that you have a horizon set, it's time to think of what could be the most appropriate strategy to meet your goal, or at least, move closer to it.

In this simple way, you can set your halfway goals every month, which are useful as a reference that will allow you to know that you're right on track.

For instance, if your chosen goal was to finish your university studies, amongst the different monthly goals you that you can write down are:

- Passing the Economy finals.
- Delivering the State and Society final project.

This way, you'll help yourself channel our daily energies, since by having small goals, so possible and achievable, investing our energy in studying and writing a project doesn't seem as far away and unattainable.

Also, you can keep subdividing our goals on the medium-term into other, easier to fulfill goals, where ambitions would be smaller and their fulfillment guides to complete our monthly goal.

Which could be:

- Reading the Economy books.
- Doing a summary.
- Re-reading the subjects.
- Re-reading a second time.
- Finding a subject for the project.
- Find partners who want to work in conjunction on your project.
  - Dividing the work.
  - Coming up with an idea for a proposal.

Every time you feel like you have nothing to do, or you think that moving forward with your work will take a lot of time and effort, you'll have a useful list that will make the small tasks easier for you to keep moving forward.

The best part of all, is that you know that despite the fact that these are small and perhaps insignificant tasks, every time you finish one successfully, you'll be one step closer from your goals.

Remember to put your lists on a strategic place, taking into account that it must be located on a visible space where you generally go to procrastinate.

This can be the corner of your television, if you're one to watch long TV shows, it can be on your personal computer, if you're one of those who prefer video games, and even as the lockscreen of your mobile device, if you're prone to spending your time on social media.

Complete your tasks quickly, this way you'll feel the pleasure of checking one more task off of your list (in time, this will become the most pleasant activity of your day).

If you've met all your weekly goals, or daily goals, you can enjoy a well-earned rest.

In case that you feel that the medium-term tasks are not working for you either, we can always keep minimizing your objectives into smaller lists.

You can even design daily lists where amongst the daily tasks you also include a schedule in which you need to perform every task.

If you're one of those people who truly struggle with making new habits, don't doubt playing dirty with your own procrastinator mind. For instance, if you set a studying time between 10 and 11 in the morning, right before lunchtime, you'll know that immediately after you finish studying you can carry on with your lunch.

Respect the list and let your mind suffer for a few days. After a couple of days, you'll start catching up and you'll get to build a very productive habit. The best part is once you've reached this stage, you'll set off on your own spiral of success that will start turning and turning in giant steps.

What is a spiral of success?

The spiral of success is what explains that successful people tend to be even more successful, while those people who've been stuck for a while in the same place, are likely to remain static for many years.

It's about a feeling of satisfaction, confidence and fulfillment that getting new achievements often provides us, which in most cases is more a matter of perception which motivates the most optimistic people to move forward.

By instance, if we start working out with the rigid objective of being able to run a 42k mile marathon, the most likely thing to happen is that when we do our first attempts and we start measuring our abilities we'll realize that with great effort, we'll only be able to keep a competitive pace for 3 or 4 miles.

At this point, there are those who start doing calculations and realize that they weren't able to complete not even a 10% of the distance necessary to become a marathon professional. That image of far away-ness and the feeling that we're moving slowly towards our goal, can really affect our goals and make us feel much less motivated to go out running the following day.

That's why making weekly and monthly lists can offer us better results, make us feel like we're inside the spiral of success and give us a boost of spirit, which in many cases can be all that it takes to start getting positive results.

If your dream is to become a marathon runner, it's okay if you want to finish the 42k mile race with a good time, but the most important thing is to be aware of our starting point, and try to impose ourselves on much more appropriate challenges for our set of skills.

For instance, on the day we find out we're only capable of completing 3k miles in really bad time, instead of worrying about how far we are from the 42k miles, we set ourselves the goal of reaching the 6k miles by the end of the month, we'll be able to gout running every morning knowing that we're not far away from our goal and that if we start running three times a week and we can add a quarter of a mile on each day, at the end of every practice, by the end of that week, we could be adding almost an extra mile. The necessary distance so that after 4 days of running, you can reach your final goal of 6k miles by the end of the month.

The best of all is after running 3k miles and a half in the second part of a race, we won't feel like losers for being so far away from our goal, but we will be left with a feeling of success and satisfaction, that will be enough motivation to get us going and make us train the following morning.

The more you feel like you're succeeding, the more confidence in yourself you'll project and the more ambitious the goals you can start setting for yourself. The more time you invest in chasing your goals, the better your skills will be, you'll learn to administrate your energies in a more efficient way, and your body will slowly adapt so that the work feels less heavy.

After some months pass by, you'll start noticing that by taking small steps you'd have gone along a great distance which separated the starting point from your most ambitious goal.

Besides, you could even start setting yourself long-term goals like running a 10 mile marathon, or 15 mile or 21 mile marathon.

Fulfilling these goals, improving your times, and perceiving the changes that will start to happen in yourself is what's known as the spiral of success, once it starts turning it'll get you really far.

Establishing a frame for work

Many times, we have the problem that our minds are used to thinking that home is a space for unraveling, and therefore, our brain it's not prepared to perform tasks that demand much effort from it.

On the other hand, when we find ourselves in the office, we generally arrive with a bigger resolution to do work, just like in university we are more prepared to do a lot of studying.

That's why, when we try studying or working from home, we're basically fighting against a habit that's been imprinted on our minds.

The best thing we can do in this case, is building a new ritual or routine, or choosing a space that explains to our brains that it's time to start working.

Until recently, I had an office to work in and I assisted the public library to study, this way the rules were clear and I knew exactly what I had to do in each space.

When the pandemic hit, both places shut their doors, and I had to start doing these things at home. Which is why, when I sat on my computer, I didn't know if I had this study work or check my social media, it was definitely a great change that I wasn't prepared for.

But in time, I started building my own spaces. On one side, I have my computer on a desk, next to my aquarium and the most comfortable chair in the house, and I took care to explain that while I'm sitting in it, it's necessary that nobody interrupts me. That way, I can fully focus on work without any kind of distraction.

On the other hand, I started printing my university annotations. This way, I can take them with me to the park, where I use my time to take some air and study for a few hours.

This is how I managed to accomplish that when I sit in a specific place, my mind is already preparing for the activity that I'm about to perform.

Resist Temptations

If the fulfillment of our goals is the engine that moves us to fulfill our dreams, temptations would be something like the important obstacles we face along the way.

Meaning, we visualize that we want to deliver our project, we sit at our desk and we open the notebooks and books, but suddenly we get an Instagram notification.

We check what happened and it's that person that we're into, they've "liked" our picture. The most likely thing to happen is that we check their page again, or we wait to see if something else happens. After a while, we choose to text them and, before we realize it, it's been 2 hours.

The way I see it, that notification would be the equivalent to a flat tire right before a very important journey. Which is why it's necessary to avoid all kinds of distractions.

Later, we'll talk about how much time dedicated to our personal enjoyment is healthy and enough, but for now, we'll focus on stopping distractions from becoming a part of our work zone.

For instance, if we know that we're prone to procrastinate every time our cell phone rings, the best thing we can do to stop the phone from becoming and anchor (just for its mere presence), is considering the choice of turning it off, or leaving it in silent mode in a different room.

With this strict measure, we know that if we want to use our phone again, our best choice is to finish our obligations as quickly as possible first.

In my case, I need my cell phone to work -but it's also very distracting- I installed an app that only lets me use certain functions while I'm on working hours.

It's called "Forest", an *app* where we plant a tree which basically renders our phone "useless", until the timer dictates it can be used again. If the timer reaches the end of the countdown, trees grow healthy and they decorate our forest. If, on the contrary, temptation is greater and you open unauthorized apps, your tree withers and dies.

Last year I managed to plant over 1200 trees on the app, which means over 600 hours of focus. So, if your phone represents a threat to your productivity, I recommend this app to you.

As I did with my cell phone, every person should make the greatest effort to step away from all that distracts them. If it's about people, you can always reason and bargain a truce for some hours.

On the other hand, if it's about something that we really enjoy, like a football game, the most advisable thing is to make a better schedule of our days and activity hours.

To stop procrastinating, it's important we organize a plan which allows us to work in an optimal way, by following a schedule that adapts to us. If we make a super tight schedule for ourselves, with a minimal time dedicated to fun and entertainment, the most likely thing to happen is that you'll abandon the ship and you won't continue with the program.

Pomodoro technique

Another recommended technique for those who excessively struggle with putting their distractions aside and focusing for long periods of time, is the technique known as the Pomodoro Clock.

This technique consists of fractionating time into short cycles so that our goal is apparently much easier to achieve. In this way, what we're looking for is to switch from a 25-minute interval of focus and productivity, to a 5-minute interval of entertainment.

Just like this, our next goal won't be the difficult task of summarizing a full book, avoiding all the distractions that could step in our way during long hours, but you'll be doing a deal with your mind, guaranteeing 5 minutes of entertainment in exchange for only 25 minutes of effort. A deal that seems more than reasonable.

What this technique strives for is that we can squeeze all of the concentration that we have to offer, and before our focus starts drifting off and we lower our performance levels, we enjoy a well-deserved break. Then, after pleasure time is over, we can get back to focusing 100% on our work.

The only exception that this renowned technique contemplates is that after two hours of work, meaning, after four cycles, we get 20 minutes of entertainment and fun.

This happens because the concentration grades are related to time, and after two hours of work, the most likely thing to happen is that our minds won't be as productive as they were at the beginning of the day. Which is why, after every fourth cycle, we are forced to take, as a minimum, a 20-minute break.

There are some rules that we must abide by, in detail, so that this technique is as effective as possible. Some of these are:

- Avoid all distractions during the 25 minutes of concentration. If you achieve this, enjoy your 5-minute break. If you don't achieve it, you'll have to start over.
- Use your breaks to do something different,

move your body, breathe a little, don't forget to hydrate and whenever you're ready, get back to your next concentration session.

- Times must be met on schedule and breaks are mandatory. It doesn't matter if you think you're doing well and you can easily keep going.

The Pomodoro technique is a deal we make with ourselves. If your mind kept its part of the bargain, you must keep yours.

The thing about this technique is that it can be a little complex when you're starting to use it, once you adapt to it, it'll be easier to administer production and entertainment times separately. What this technique aims for, is to make us give our 100% in both things, no middle points. Either we're focused or we're not.

As we start owning this technique, there will come a time in which we can divide our tasks in Pomodoro cycles and not in hours anymore. Causing our to-do lists to perfect and be more and more efficient.

For instance:

- 10hs: Study for two Pomodoro.
- 14hs: Work on the pending work deliveries for six Pomodoro.
- 17hs: Go out jogging for three Pomodoro.

Administer your energies

Another means to get better results, when it comes to productivity, is being able to know ourselves a little more. This way we can calculate how much effort we can demand from ourselves, and which schedules are best to do so.

Generally, when we have more or less defined sleeping schedules, our body tends to activate quickly, reaching a peak of productivity, maintaining itself at a hundred percent of its energy during some hours, and then it starts to decline. When the time comes, our concentration, our will strength and our generalized tiredness will tell us to stop and let us know it's time to go to bed.

That's why having regular schedules tends to be effective when chasing goals and trying to fulfill them. Now, regulating our schedules will do little if we insist on placing as the last activity of the day, our work and study times.

In doing so, you'd be demanding your mind efficiency in a moment where it doesn't have that much to offer, and you'll have to constantly fight the urge to go to sleep.

That's why it's recommended to start the day off with what seems more difficult. In this way, when demanding your body and mind to step up to your goals, you'll have bigger energy reserves to face every day struggles. Your tasks can be postponed a little bit more than planned, but you'll be covered, since not even sleep or tiredness will be an issue.

The best of all is that, if by lunch time you manage to perform the most tedious and important tasks, you'll get to enjoy the rest of the day more calmly. You'll be completely free of guilt and you'll feel a positive satisfaction that will act as fuel so that the next day you try to repeat your accomplishments.

Besides, if by the end of the day you have tasks that demand a lesser amount of energy, or that turn out to be more enjoyable, the most likely thing is that you'll do them anyway. As we know, it is not the same thing to make it to the night and think we still have to do our thesis research, than to simply make it to the night knowing we have to water the plants.

Finally, this way of administering your times and tasks will give you a wider window to adapt to new proposals which you didn't plan, but that can come up. If a friend invites you to a party, or if your partner won two tickets to the movies, or any other event that could happen, it's not the same thing to find out once you're already enjoying your free time, to find out at 6 in the afternoon, when you still haven't done your homework and you still haven't gone to the gym.

Get inspired by triumphant people and follow in the footsteps

When I was a little boy, I always looked up to the characters of my favorite stories. And as a Sci-Fi lover, I started to aspire to be more like Johnny Rico, from the book *Starship Troopers* one day, more like commander Ciricco, from *Titan*, or like Paul Atreides, from *Dune*.

That's why when I was little, I ran and crawled along a plain that extended and covered an entire block in front of my house, always carrying a plastic gun with me. I knew that if one day we had to fight aliens on a far away planet, I'd be the first one to join the fight along the lines of the planetary army.

Fortunately, so far, we haven't had any conflicts with any alien race. But still, it's extraordinary to see how our everyday activities can be coordinated in order to follow in the footsteps of a reference.

Once I realized that I was born too soon to fight

in space, I started thinking that training my body and fight skills was all for nothing, and I started abandoning those practices.

Then, I started finding my inspiration in many other idols, which helped me guide my steps. Frank Herbert, Isaac Asimov, Gabriel García Márquez, all renowned writers that manage to breathe life into incredible characters, extraordinary worlds and stories that, still to this day I keep looking up to and reliving.

But as it was expected, none of them was born as a great writer. On the contrary, I found out that every single one of them started their journey from very early on working on local newspapers, writing articles, columns and short stories that cemented the grounds of their writing skills.

That's how, just like them, I started banging on every newspaper's and journalistic media's door that I could find in my way, until finally, one gave me the opportunity to work as a journalist. Even if, at the beginning, I started writing every once in a while, for free, before a semester had passed, I had already managed to get a new informational position that belonged to the same company.

Today, I'm still not as known as my references. But their lives continue to guide my steps and I hope that someday my books are a part of some young dreamer's library, like their works are a part of mine.

Find groups that power your skills

When starting on a path, the least we need are people around us who try to put obstacles in our way and turn into a ballast, stopping us in our tracks.

In many cases, the mind of a procrastinator is poisoned by the comments of those who surround them. Those, skewed by a pessimistic or conformist view of life, terrify them with comments that far from pushing them to chase their dreams, plant fears and a heavy feeling so that they conform with what they already have.

On the contrary, those who mingle with people who inspire us with a greater amount of confidence, tend to go further, since we don't feel as much fear when gambling on our own projects or sailing on a new adventure.

Today, thanks to social media, you can find all kinds of groups. In those communities, you can often find a warm environment, where mutual help can benefit those who don't know quite clearly how to move forward.

You can find every kind of group, and feeling included in them is quite beneficial, since you start to know more success stories, and the that you might not have contemplate in your reality. Besides, you'll probably get support and congratulations in each positive step you manage to take, as long as you make the choice to share them with the community.

You don't have to be afraid to share ideas, you don't have to believe that everyone out there is looking for a way to take advantage of us. If we want to grow as people and move forward towards our goals, it's important to be able to trust those who surround us. And if you can't do it, perhaps it means it's time to meet new people, maybe, if you're lucky you'll manage to find an *accountability buddy* willing to accompany you on your journey.

What is an *accountability buddy*?

An *accountability buddy* is a partner which we tell all our projects, and everything we intend to do every week, too.

This way, since we know that every week, we'll have the duty and obligation to talk to that person again, we'll be moved by the motivation to do something, to get a new result or a significant breakthrough in our path. That way, we'll have some novelty that will make our partner happier and which will motivate them to continue moving towards their own goals.

In general, no one wants to call a person to tell them they couldn't keep moving forward with their project, making excuses week after week. That's why having someone to trust, to share our goals with and whom we choose to start an *accountability buddy* type of relationship with, can be more than enough motivation so that we never stop chasing our dreams.

While it often happens among partners who do the same kind of activities, that's not a requirement. It only has to be someone with whom you have the certainty that you can sincerely speak to about your aspirations, desires and dreams, and someone you can rely on.

They have to be able to bring new and fresh ideas when we find ourselves stuck on a dead end. Many times it happens that, when trying to find a specific solution, we start focusing more and more on a problem. Perhaps we don't see that there is a detour which will allow us to take an easier road.

"*When NASA started sending astronauts to space, they realized that pens didn't work on zero gravity.*

After investing several millions of dollars and two years of running tests, the space agency developed a pen that could write in space, upside down, and on nearly every surface, in temperatures that went from -80 to 65 Celsius degrees.

When faced with the same obstacle, the Russians used a pencil.

It's also useful that this person has their own ambitions and that are capable of achieving positive results. This way, we'll be forced to step up our game, haunted by the idea that someone else will get to where we wanted to get. But that, at the same time, are capable of being tough enough to tell us when they think we're not putting out enough of ourselves to chase our dreams.

Advice:

To make sure your *accountability buddy* relationship is truly productive, the most important thing is that the contact happens weekly, without skipping. The best thing is that it's not always the same one who calls, but that every week at the same time the contact happens, because it makes it clear that they're both interested and they benefit from this relationship.

On the other hand, we should try not to choose people of affinity, it can even turn out that a stranger we know nothing about is more useful, because if we choose a friend or a partner, they can probably take pity on us, be soft until we reach a point where we actually don't care about what they think of us.

Don't be hesitant about sharing your lists, medium-term and long-term objectives, and try to empower each other in those moments where you're both motivated, accept all the possible help when your buddy is achieving better results than yours, encourage them and give them strength, whenever you're the one who's doing better.

It does little good to be stubborn and choose to

move forward on our own, in this type of relationship nobody is nobody's mentor, but they're like two mountain climbers joined by a rope. Don't hesitate to pull on it all that you need to so that your partner starts going up, at some point they'll do the same for us, and that way, you'll both make it to the top.

Reward yourself for your triumphs

The best part about having productive days and ending procrastination is that, despite the fact that we're going to invest more and more time in productive tasks, this doesn't mean that we're going to have less fun, or feel like we're losing when it comes to recreation or entertainment.

In fact, it's the opposite: by not procrastinating, not only are we segmenting productive hours so that we truly take advantage of them, but we are doing the same thing with leisure time. The difference is that we wouldn't be looking for it in small and meaningless actions, like checking our social media or watching YouTube videos. The goal is that we start taking the most advantage possible from it, by doing things that we actually enjoy.

Which means, if we start increasing our productivity, we'll be able to get some free time earlier, whether it's by the end of the day or by the end of each week. Thanks to this, we'll have more time and freedom to reward ourselves for our efforts and do those things that actually make us happy.

Like I mentioned in the first part of this book, I'm a person who enjoys camping a lot, but I know it's an activity that demands too much time.

Also, I like going out for a beer at the park or at a bar that has exterior tables, but I know that in order to do so, I need to fulfill all my daily goals on schedule.

It's important that we focus on those things that we like to do so that they act as inspiration, to sit down and get to work when we are wasting time on actions that don't satisfy us enough.

In my experience, before I started optimizing my performance, I spent long hours of my day watching *streams* of *Age of Empire 2*, managing to waste up to 5 hours of my day doing so.

Of course, I like watching the games of *Age of Empire 2*, but if I put this on a scale, it doesn't come close to the pleasure I feel when I go to the movies or go camping.

Then, why invest so many hours watching games of Age of Empire 2?

The answer is simple, since going to the movies or grabbing a couple of beers demanded, as a minimum, three hours of my time. And I knew that with a collapsed schedule, I couldn't afford to do it.

Anyway, I couldn't go camping on the weekends, since I had postponed my obligations so much, on Saturdays and Sundays I had to dedicate my time to my university studies.

I never had the time, neither could I do what I truly wanted to do. Putting off your obligations not only implies that your academic and work performances fall apart, but also your quality of life in general.

That's why it's so recommended to start rewarding ourselves for our efforts. We can even write down the activities that we enjoyed the most in the same list of our weekly activities. In this way, we know that if our procrastination doesn't allow us to keep up with our schedule, it's those activities that we like to do the ones who'll be in jeopardy.

Work with your time so that you can go to the stadium to watch your favorite team's game on Sunday, or go out *karting*, or fishing. Something that you really enjoy.

You can also give yourself short-term rewards; finish your activities and watch a movie, or go out to the park to have a burger.

If we get used to the fact that the rewards are the consequence of good actions, we'll start feeling motivated to finish our commitments earlier each time.

Just like that, we'll also feel like the activities are more satisfying than ever. Not only will we be doing something that we appreciate, but we will be living it as a reward, which adds a symbolic and very important value to it.

Have you ever seen how people who are partying at a bar have so much fun? In their faces, you can often appreciate a certain joy that exceeds that moment, it's much larger than beer, the place or the friends that are with them.

You can see reflected on their faces the accomplishments achieved after long hours of work, months of sacrifice and a lot of personal satisfaction.

The opposite; is being home watching short YouTube videos, 'cause we know that we still have many tasks to do. The most common thing is that we do it feeling an inner guilt that is so strong, it barely lets us enjoy the video.

Think about it carefully, the dogs who do tricks, the mules who carry the loads and the messenger pigeons are often fed after they do their work, never before.

We're not that different. In this case, we must be the ones to put the carrot in front of our own face as a motivation to force us to move forward.

Rethink what we do

In the renowned book "*The 7 Habits of Highly Effective People*", Stephen R. Covey explains that a method to start making our lives much more productive, is to apply an activities segmentation, which will allow us to set our priorities in a better way. If we use it with wisdom, it can generate an important change in habits that will make us more efficient people.

The chart is composed of four quadrants which are organized based on two variables, it will allow us to classify all our daily activities.

The (Y) axis is composed of the "Important" and "Unimportant" variables, in a way that we can put on top those activities that we think will affect us in a greater measure if we don't perform them. This can be finishing our projects, going to work, spending time with our family, meeting up with friends, etc.

On the other hand, on the bottom part of the chart we can put those activities that we do and that are meaningless to our life: checking social media, watching television, spending time with people who don't bring anything positive to our lives, etc.

However, the (X) axis at the "Urgent" and "Non-urgent" variables, which are classified based on whether the task that we have to do must be resolved right away or not. Which means, spending time with our friends and family it's not something urgent, what is though, is answering our social media messages, picking up phone calls or preparing a delivery which is overdue.

Once we have written down our activities, and have classified them in our chart, which we'll call "priority matrix", we'll have a much clearer picture regarding what we must do, in which moment and if we really want to do it.

For instance, if you have to do something that is considered important but not urgent, it's only a matter of scheduling a date in the calendar so that you can finish that activity when you really have the time to work on it.

If the task, however, is important and urgent, the best thing to do is to start working on it immediately and without interruptions.

With interruptions we mean, probably, things that aren't important but that are also urgent. In many opportunities, these are like obstacles for our concentration. The most common things in this field can be social media notifications, meetings with people who don't bring a lot to our lives and even keeping up with the results of some sport.

Even if these are things that generally can't wait, because they're happening right in the moment, it's necessary that we are clever enough to know when to put them aside, and even start dedicating less and less time to them.

The same happens with activities that aren't important, but that aren't urgent either, like watching a series on Netflix, performing some extracurricular activities that we committed to, even though they don't really add a lot to our lives, returning calls, etc.

The major goal of this chart is that the fields "Important" and "Urgent" are always empty, as long as it's possible. And that when there's something in there, we put all our resources into satisfyingly fulfilling those activities.

Generally, those fields are the ones that we give the least importance to. But if we look to perfect what we do, and transform into successful people, they have to be the points in which we invest the most energy in.

A lot of people know that they have to finish their career, study a Master's, learn a new language, find a new job or more important clients. But since urgency isn't beating them up, they often postpone those activities longer than necessary, sometimes even for years.

The opposite happens with those things that we classify within "Least important", which if we do or don't do them, they won't affect our lives at all, or maybe they'll do so negatively. This is a section of the chart which we must look at carefully and with a critical eye.

For instance, I spent long years in a group that I shared with my high school partners, I read their messages, I went to the reunions and I shared moments with them just because I saw that everyone was doing it, and it was considered the right thing to do.

One day I realized that despite the fact that it had been important at some point of my life -or not- I didn't care anymore about anything they did, talking to them didn't satisfy me nor did it bring any benefits, so I proceeded to exit the group and then my relationship with them, allowing me to use that time and energy in other activities that were more interesting to me.

It's important that the things that we do, really help us become the people we want to be, or that simply entertain us. For instance, it happened to me when I realized that football wasn't a sport that I liked at all, despite dedicating every Sunday afternoon to it.

In that same line of thought, I didn't like going out dancing that much either, but ever since I was seventeen until I was twenty-two, I did it because it seemed like going to clubs, getting drunk and investing large amounts of money on tickets was necessary to obtain quality entertainment.

Now that I'm somewhere around thirty years old, I rather do ice skating, get together and play some board games or go camping. I'm not saying those activities are better or more fun than the previous ones, but at least I know that I'm doing them because they add something to my life, and that's really important.

Create new habits

Once we are aware of those things that we want to incorporate to our lives, and those we don't, there will come the time to start the slow process of building new habits.

Like I mentioned earlier, mental energy is not an infinite good and every new activity you choose to incorporate into your life will demand an important mental energy quota, something that our brain won't be comfortable with at all.

After all, the brain, like all of us, only wants to do its every day job and spend the least amount of energy possible to do so, which means forcing it to work extra hours won't be easy at all.

This is where the most amount of thoughts that lead us to procrastinate are born, because the brain will start using its best tricks so that we quit trying to impose this new change in our lives. At the end of the day, the brain's duty is to keep us alive. And if doing things the way it has been doing them has fulfilled its goal so far, it doesn't need to make a change.

To make us quit, the first mechanism it will use will be evasive thoughts, which consists of a bombing of excuses that seek to make us give up on our initiative.

If it's creative enough, those excuses will be interpreted by us as real obstacles and it will make us rethink if we really need to make the change.

But we must be stronger than that. If we make the decision that the best thing for our lives is to go out running each morning, we'll have to stick firmly to that position and go out running, even if our minds are not happy with the decision.

A strategy that I recommend to avoid excuses easily, is to write them down in a notebook. This way, every time we come up with a reason why we can't go out running, we'll simply jot it down. Then, we'll start becoming aware that what we see as obstacles, are actually mere excuses that aim to make us fail our goals.

In the future, when one of them crosses our minds, we'll automatically know that this evasive thought is a simple excuse. Being aware of it, we'll know that it's not an obstacle that's stopping us, it's not being strong enough.

This way we won't be satisfied with the choice to not go out for a run, and we'll have more tools to defeat the obstacles that our mind sets for us, doing the activity anyway.

If we're strong enough and we start defeating our minds repetitively and systematically, our brain will understand that its voice is not being heard. If it wants to save energy, it will have to come up with a new completely automated system which will allow it to do what you want without exceeding; that's called making a habit.

The best example of a habit that I can think of right now is typing on the computer. Probably, the first time you did it, it demanded an incredible amount of focus and mental energy. You had to know the position of each letter, think of which finger you had to use for each one, return the hand to the same place every time and adapt to the following key. A very complex job, in which nine of the ten fingers are moving independently and in coordination to type quickly and efficiently. Something that, if it were done consciously, it would drain our mental energy in minutes.

But, by forcing the brain to do it over and over again, in time, it will remember the keys' positions and make each finger's movements automatic, and create an effective system and coordination that will allow us to simply write without thinking about it.

I don't know how you do with this typing thing, but the same probably happens to you when you drive a car or when you brush your teeth.

If we manage to make the brain stop resisting and make a habit of what we want to do, it will stop making up excuses and consume so much mental energy, which will make it easier and easier every day.

How to be successful when building our habits

I already told you the first recommendation, which is to be aware of the fact that excuses aren't real obstacles, and do our best to ignore them.

The second recommendation is to be persistent and to do the activity regularly for at least the first 21 times, which is the estimated time it takes to create a new habit. Of course, it doesn't have to be exact, but if your goal is to go running three times a week, put a special focus on not skipping a single session for the first seven weeks.

Another recommendation is to try and add a certain regularity to the schedule and create a previous routine before performing the activity. What this will do is, when we start preparing ourselves, our mind and body will start understanding and preparing to perform the action.

Then remember the effort it took the first time that you did it, and compare it to the effort it took the last few times. There probably exists an important improvement when it comes to the strength of will that it took you to get going.

Finally, learn to be disciplined and do things because you consciously know that it's the best thing for your life, and not because your brain reads it that way. Generally, the brain uses a never-ending bag of tricks so that we do what it wants, although it's not always right.

If we start a diet, it may start demanding that we feed ourselves and make us feel like we really need to, even if we know that we don't. That is why we have to be disciplined and always be a step forward of our impulses and instincts.

But this doesn't mean that the feelings of thirst, hunger or tiredness aren't useful, because they've managed to keep us alive for a long time. But it's important to understand that as of today, we leave immersed in a social construct that our body doesn't fully interpret. Which is why, it's us who have to lead the way for our body and teach it that it's us who will be in charge, and that we're not willing to give in to the most primitive and natural impulses.

Use procrastination to your advantage

In case you're trying to make your life take on a new direction, but despite your efforts, it seems like sterile activities seduce you and drag you into procrastination, there is a resource that you can use so you can make a 360° spin in your life.

It's about placing obstacles between you and those activities that tend to lead you to procrastinate, and clear the way towards the productive activities in which you'd like to invest the most amount of time.

A clear example of this is when we get to our home, we sit on the sofa and quickly, before asking ourselves what it is that we truly want to do, we turn the TV on and we spend a lot of hours watching TV shows that mean nothing to us, or else we start checking our social media in our cell phones. This happens because it's quicker and simpler to execute these actions, instead of getting ready to start a different activity.

If, on the contrary, we had to go to a cyber cafe to access our social media, or if the TV was in a different room and we had to go get it before we sat in front of it, we'd most likely dedicate less time to these activities.

Of course, we don't have to go to the extreme, but yes, we can start imposing certain concrete actions, like removing the batteries from the remote control and keeping it away in some drawer in the kitchen, or getting home and leaving our cell phone on a distant shelf, very far away from us.

In this way, when we sit on the sofa and we don't know what to do, we won't have the option to start wasting time so easily. Instead, we'd have to invest some seconds and a little bit of effort to do it, which will give us more time to think if we really want to focus on doing some of this stuff.

Now, if we added to this the possibility to get a book closer to the sofa, it wouldn't be so strange to consider the option of reading a few chapters, just because we have to invest little effort to start said activity.

Similar to what happens when we go to the dentist and we find a mountain of old magazines. Surely, reading them isn't part of what you like to do, what entertains you nor what you would consider productive. But "they're right there", so we simply do it.

With a similar logic, we can release all of the obstacles that keep us away from the activities that we have trouble doing, and place them between us and our favorite non-productive activities.

There are some examples, many of which are too extreme, that I started imposing throughout my life, but that gave me many results.

One of them was living alone in a residence where I didn't have access to the internet. That way, every time I came to my home, I was incredibly bored, which pushed me to do all kinds of stuff.

In those two years that I lived without access to the internet, I got incredible grades at university, I visited over fifteen museums, I read over fifty books, I periodically assisted a group in which they only spoke English and others where they played board games.

Those were the two most productive years of my life and, paradoxically, they were also the years where I gave up one of the most important tools for the development of my life.

Of course, I continued to have access to the internet, but only at university, in a way that I had the possibility to walk all the way there to do all my projects and print the necessary material. But when it came to doing recreational activities, I had to figure something out. The internet wasn't a choice.

This way of living without having a connection to the internet, nor a television at home was imposed by myself during a year-and-a-half that I lived in a residence and the first months after I moved to an apartment with my partner. Even though she understood that distractions weren't good for me, after half a year, she convinced me that the internet connection was in fact necessary for our lives. So, I agreed to hire the service again, as long as we didn't have a television at home (a measure she agreed to and that remains valid).

Now that I work and I study from the comfort of my home, using a computer, I'm aware that it could turn into a procrastinating tool in the blink of an eye. Which is why I've been using new self-regulation techniques that allow me to focus a hundred percent on my work, practically making me forget about those websites that took too much time away from me.

Small obstacles

The best way I found to not fall into temptation to check my social media while I did my work, was creating two different users in my computer: the first of them, focused on work. With it, I have access to necessary tools to write news, find information and not much more.

I even blocked social media and some news websites that I read in the morning. I took everything out, and I personalized the user with inspiring *wallpapers*. I know that the user is created purely, and exclusively to do work.

On the other hand, if I want to get distracted for a couple of minutes, checking the news, or checking social media, I have to log out and open the user that was created for recreational purposes.

Switching back and forth from the different users is not something that takes more than fifty seconds, but those fifty seconds are more annoying than the three seconds it would take me to open Instagram or Facebook from the browser I use to do my work. Basically, it gives me the time to think if I really need, or want to check my social media.

After some months pass by, you'll get used to not wasting time and the temptation simply disappears.

Conclusion

As you might've noticed throughout this book, I am not a psychologist, I am not rich, nor do I run a company that's valued in millions of dollars abroad; but I am a dreamer, a person who lived its entire life filled with ambitions and that has the necessary will power to chase every single one of their dreams, as far away and absurd as they might seem.

I would love to tell you that chasing my dreams has been an experience filled with triumphs and that I never doubted that I'd be able to fulfill my goals. The truth is, my path was constantly besieged by a million distractions which made me believe that my existence wasn't worth a single thing, and that I'd never be nothing more than a vicious person, all because I spent entire days playing online games without having enough will to finish a single project.

I suffered a hundred times over the guilt of procrastination and every time I lied down, I felt a profound depression thinking of all those things that I hadn't done. I spent long hours awake, thinking that I had to gain back control over my life and I programmed a large number of activities to do the next morning, but again I fell in a trap that had the potential to steal entire months away from me.

If there's something in my path that I do appreciate and that I want to share with you, is that every time I hit rock bottom, I had the courage to recognize the problem and to walk the extra mile in order to move on and overcome the obstacle that didn't let me move forward towards my dreams.

To finish the first of my university careers, I chose to turn off my cell phone and keep it in a drawer from which it didn't come out for the following two years. I still remember my friends laughing at me because I was the only person that kept calling them to their landline, or that went visiting without calling first, knocking at their doors.

If we put together the two years I lived without a cell phone and the two years I spent without an internet connection, it would be four years in which I had to step away and give up the commodities that the 21st century has to offer us, only because I didn't know how to handle an issue.

I probably saw it as a solution at that moment, but I was only covering the sun with my hand. Sooner or later, technology was going to be a part of my life and it would remind me again that change had to happen within me. Even if it seems easy, we can't escape our weaknesses forever.

I started applying every strategy that I mentioned in this book, and every single one of them was working out for me. Of course, they were working, but no magical formulas. Every time I applied the Pomodoro Technique, I managed to fulfill my goals. Every time I told my *accountability buddy* about a project, I was able to give a hundred percent of myself to carry on with it.

I managed to build new habits, I learned to wake up early and finish all of my obligations before noon. But every time, I have to remind myself of the kind of person that I want to become, and seduce myself with outings and camping trips, so I can stay on the productivity track.

I still don't have the necessary strength to have video games installed on my computer and not spend whole days wasting my time on them. But I do have the sense to choose not to have them.

I don't guarantee you that you'll never procrastinate again using these strategies. I can't even guarantee you that I won't procrastinate again eventually.

What I do know is that some years ago my life was a mess, without a set course, and that I'm becoming more and more aware of what I want to achieve in this life, and of the path that I have to take so I can get there. But, the most important thing, I also learned to recognize the things that keep me away from that goal.

I hope this book allows you to identify if you are actually procrastinating. And that, of all the strategies I shared, there is one or several that give you that necessary push so you can start reducing these issues and do more in your productive hours. This way, you'll manage to become the person whom you've always wanted to be.

Thank you for buying this book. The copyright is exclusive property of the author, therefore, the reproduction, copying and distribution of this book are not allowed, whether it's for commercial or non-profit purposes.

If this manual was useful to you, I'd really appreciate it if you could rate it on Amazon. Your support helps me continue writing.

www.ingramcontent.com/pod-product-compliance
Lightning Source LLC
Chambersburg PA
CBHW072235230526
45466CB00024B/1927